Hope For Tough Times

Robert H. Schuller

Thomas Nelson Publishers
Nashville · Camden · New York

Selections in this book are from *Tough Times Never Last, But Tough People Do!* by Robert H. Schuller, published by Thomas Nelson Publishers.

Copyright © 1983 Robert H. Schuller

All rights reserved. Written permission must be secured from the publisher to use or reproduce any part of this book, except for brief quotations in critical reviews or articles.

Published in the United States of America.

Scripture quotations in this publication are from The New King James Version. Copyright © 1979, 1980, 1982, Thomas Nelson, Inc., Publishers.
ISBN 0-8407-5346-2

The lyrics quoted from *South Pacific* on page 11 are copyright © 1949 by Richard Rodgers and Oscar Hammerstein. Copyright renewed, Williamson Music Co., owner of publication and allied rights for the Western Hemisphere and Japan. International copyright secured. All rights reserved. Used by permission.

Hope
is holding on,
praying expectantly,
never giving up

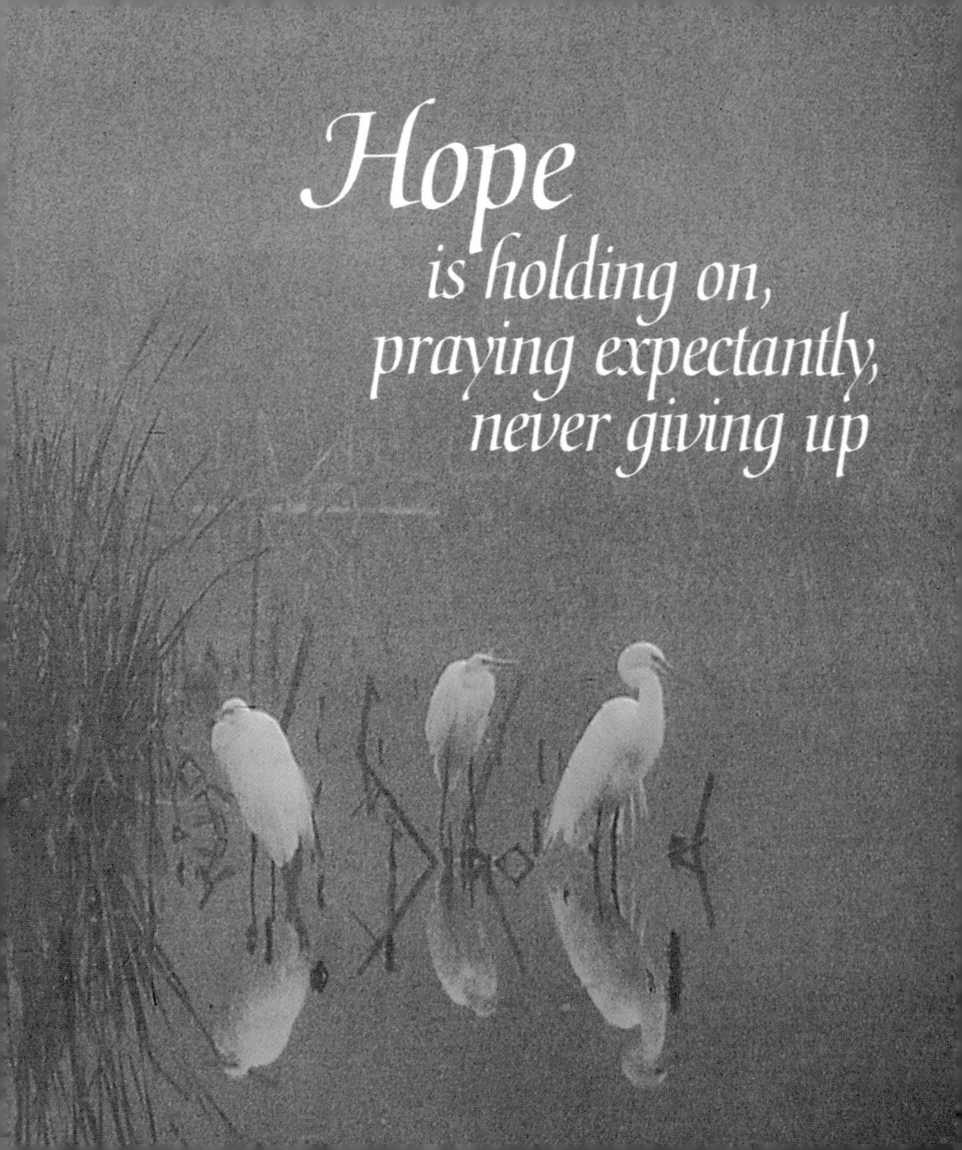

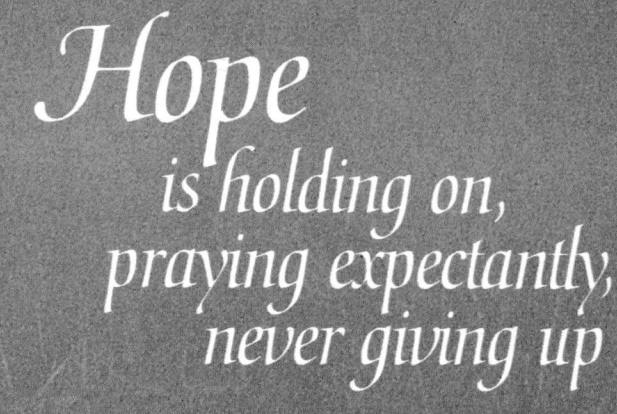

For I know the thoughts that I think toward you, says the LORD, thoughts of peace and not of evil, to give you a future and a hope.

JEREMIAH 29:11

A Cockeyed Optimist

I recently received a beautiful letter from a person I have admired from a distance. Six times Mary Martin's picture appeared on the cover of *Life* magazine. America loved her as Peter Pan, as Nellie Forbush in "South Pacific," and as Maria Von Trapp in the original Broadway production of "Sound of Music."

I saw her as a person who was always positive, joyous, optimistic, and happy. I never understood or knew the personal tragic paths she had walked quietly and had faced prayerfully.

"Three times in the past nine years your

ministry has deeply changed my life," she wrote. Later, over lunch, she said, "The principles of possibility thinking helped me accept the loss of my beloved husband nine years ago. That was a tough time, believe me!

"Then I lost my voice and was unable to sing. That was like losing my life. Then one morning a possibility-thinking message inspired an idea that led me to health again. My singing voice returned!"

Sparkling with joy as she shared the event, she looked almost as young and attractive at sixty-nine as she must have looked when she was a bright, young starlet beginning her career. I could hardly believe she had come out of the hospital only weeks before, following a car crash that had claimed one life and almost two others.

Along with her dear friend, Janet Gaynor, and her manager, Ben Washer, she had stepped into a cab in San Francisco.

"Ben insisted, 'Please get in first, Mary.' I obliged. 'You're next,' Ben said to Janet, who slipped in the middle of the back seat. Then Ben, like a gentleman, followed and closed the door behind him. Because of this seating arrangement, Ben bore the immediate impact of the speeding car, driven by a drunken driver who ran a red light. The impact was horrible! Ben was killed and Janet spent month after torturing month lingering near death.

"I think maybe that was one of my toughest times," Mary Martin said. Without losing the twinkle, she continued, "But as you say, tough times never last, but tough people do. And I'm a tough Texan, you know!

"Richard Rodgers told me that he wrote the song, 'Cockeyed Optimist' for me! He was writing the play 'South Pacific' and he said to me, 'Mary, when I knew you'd be playing the part of Nellie, I simply thought about you and

wrote these words: "I'm only a cockeyed optimist. I am stuck like a dope with a thing called hope, and I can't get it out of my head."'"

That's the spirit that heals all diseases, redeems lives from destruction, and brings sunshine back after the rain. Tough people have it. They have hope. They can weather the worst storm. They can rough out the toughest times. They win! They come out on top.

Plan to make your dream a reality

*You can be anything
you want to be,
you can go anywhere
from where you are
if you are willing to
dream big and
work hard*

The Power of Hope

Carol Lovell is alive today because she had hope. Doctors attribute her survival after five bullet wounds in the head to hope, as much as to anything else.

On September 4, 1981, Carol went to work early at the restaurant where she was employed as a bookkeeper. The building was empty, and she let herself in with her key. Soon Carol heard a knock at the door and recognized the man who was the new custodian.

After she opened the door to him, he began slapping her around and demanded that she open the safe: "You're gonna be dead if you don't open the safe."

So, Carol opened the safe and gave him the money. *Now,* she thought, *he has what he's come for. He'll leave.*

But, the man was not done with Carol. He pulled her into the employee restroom, raped her, and shot her twice in the head.

Somehow, Carol maintained consciousness. Sure that her wounds would kill her, she prayed, "Lord, help me. I don't know how to die. I'm afraid. Give me the strength to die. Show me how." And then suddenly, she was able to pull herself to her feet. She thought, *I want to live; I don't want to die.* She ran to the front of the restaurant, and picked up the wrong phone, only to realize that she could not call out. She panicked when she realized her mistake, ran back to the office, and called a friend. She was asking her to call an ambulance when the man returned.

Seeing Carol, he shot her three more times. She fell to the floor, where she lay until the police and ambulance arrived.

She remained alert and amazingly calm as she described her attacker and informed the emergency attendants that she was wearing contact lenses. She was so calm, in fact, that the doctors felt freer to take time to determine the best way to remove the bullets from her head.

Her sister, Linda, arrived and began to fill her mind with hope and positive instructions. She told Carol, "You're going to be O.K. You're going to make it. Don't let your brain swell. Don't let your body bleed."

Amazingly, her brain never did swell, a common reaction to such a brain injury.

For weeks as Carol lay in intensive care, her sisters continued to feed her with positive thoughts and Scripture verses.

After six months of surgery, recovery, and therapy, Carol was walking and talking as she had before the accident. Her only residual difficulty after her attack has been an arm that tends to be uncooperative.

Carol's survival is incredible. She attributes her healing to hope. "Only prayer and positive thinking kept me going!"

Tough times never last, but tough people do. If you want to succeed, if you want to conquer, then *hope*—*h*old *o*n, *p*raying *e*xpectantly!

*When you've exhausted
 all possibilities remember this*

You haven't!

Tower of Hope

My first visit to Korea was right after the Korean War. Never have I seen such a bleak, barren, and defeated land. Not a single tree, shrub, or other greenery graced the landscape. All living vegetation had been consumed in order to preserve human life. Those were tough times in Korea!

Among the impoverished refugees that fled from the North were throngs of Christians who believed in a God who would never forsake those who never forsook Him. So they held onto their hope in God. One young Korean minister from that impoverished land received a scholarship to Fuller Seminary in California. While Sundo Kim was studying there he visited our church.

Imagine how impressed he must have been to see the thirteen-story tower and the large modern sanctuary with fountains! He heard and believed the principle, "Believe it and you can achieve it." He began to dream that someday he would build a church like that in Korea.

Four years ago, I returned to Korea and Sundo Kim asked me to speak in his church. All he had was a tent, but he and his people were excited. I said I'd be honored to preach in his tent on Saturday night. But Saturday morning, the telephone call came. My daughter Carol had been seriously injured in a motorcycle accident. My wife and I got on the first plane, and so I wasn't able to keep my commitment.

Recently I returned to Seoul, Korea, and my young minister friend wrote, "Dr. Schuller, four years ago you promised to speak at my church. You broke the promise—for a good reason—but this time you must stop and see my church."

Although I was scheduled to be in Korea for only forty-eight hours, I promised him that somehow I would make it to his church.

I was amazed when I arrived. The difference four years had made was incredible. We flew into a beautiful airport that is a spectacular piece of architecture, surrounded by a glorious park of lawns, trees, and waterfalls. A beautiful hotel has been reconstructed in downtown Seoul with sidewalks of polished granite and a circular driveway veneered in ceramic tile. As we drove down the magnificent new freeway that slices through Seoul, I saw it! Looming in the sky was a replica of our Garden Grove, California, Tower of Hope—fourteen stories tall, with a cross on top! And next to it was a glorious new church building with four thousand seats.

The young pastor showed me through his church, introduced me to his elders and deacons, and shared with me that he has over twelve thousand members.

It is amazing what God can do if we will give Him a little time to work His plan out! In four

years' time a band of one thousand poor
Christians with little more than hope moved
from a tent on an abandoned acre of ground in
Seoul, Korea, to a four-thousand-seat cathedral.
Today they are the world's largest United
Methodist church!

Today's decisions are tomorrow's realities

Count to Ten and Win!

Many years ago I discovered a formula for solving insolvable problems. The formula has never failed me.

In 1955, I was on my way to California to begin a new church, but we had no place to meet. In a café in Albuquerque, New Mexico, I picked up a paper napkin, and wrote the numerals "1" to "10" vertically on the left side of the paper. I let my imagination run wild. My list looked like this:

1. Rent a school building.
2. Rent a Masonic Hall.
3. Rent an Elk's Lodge.
4. Rent a mortuary chapel.
5. Rent an empty warehouse.
6. Rent a community club building.
7. Rent a Seventh-Day Adventist church.
8. Rent a Jewish synagogue.
9. Rent a drive-in theater.
10. Rent an empty piece of ground, a tent, and folding chairs.

Suddenly what had seemed totally impossible now seemed possible. Suddenly the word *impossible* sounded irresponsible, extreme, reactionary, and unintelligent.

This list was my first rudimentary effort in playing a game that I would play many times in the next thirty years. I had made my list. I then proceeded to check out each of my possibilities. It wasn't until I explored possibility nine, that I met with success. The rest is history.

When you adopt such game-playing attitudes, you generate a mental climate conducive to creativity. This is the secret behind the possibility-thinking game, "Count to Ten and Win."

When uttered aloud, the word *impossible* is devastating in its effect. Thinking stops. Progress is halted. Doors slam shut. Research comes to a screeching halt. Further experimentation is torpedoed. Projects are abandoned. Dreams are discarded.

But, let someone utter the magic words *It's possible*. Those stirring words penetrate into the subconscious tributaries of the mind, challenging and calling those proud powers to turn on and turn out new ideas! Buried dreams are resurrected. Sparks of fresh enthusiasm flicker, then burst into new flame. Lights go on again in the darkened laboratories. Telephones start ringing. Typewriters make clattering music. "Help Wanted" signs are hung out. New markets open. A great new era of adventure, experimentation, expansion, and prosperity is born.

   Here's how you, too, can play the possibility-thinking game.

Rule number one: Begin by believing you possess latent gifts of creativity. You will respect, trust, and admire your own thoughts. *Every* person can be creative.

Rule number two: Don't play it alone. Play it with problem-solving people. Play it with people who have a record of achievement and success. You *can* play it alone. But a lot of ideas might come from others.

All it takes is one idea to solve an impossible problem! Count to ten and win.

The single most important healing force is hope

An Extraordinary Determination

In the 1930s, for reasons we never understood, the normal spring rainfall never came to our Iowa farm to moisten the newly planted corn and oats. The few precious dollars that my father was able to save had to be spent on seed corn.

In the springs of 1931, 1932, and 1933, my father took all that he had left—the kernels of corn, the last cups of oats—and planted them in the ground of his small Iowa farm, expecting that the rains would fall. He hoped that the seeds would become wet and bloated until they erupted with new life, sending their tender little sprouts up through the softened spring soil.

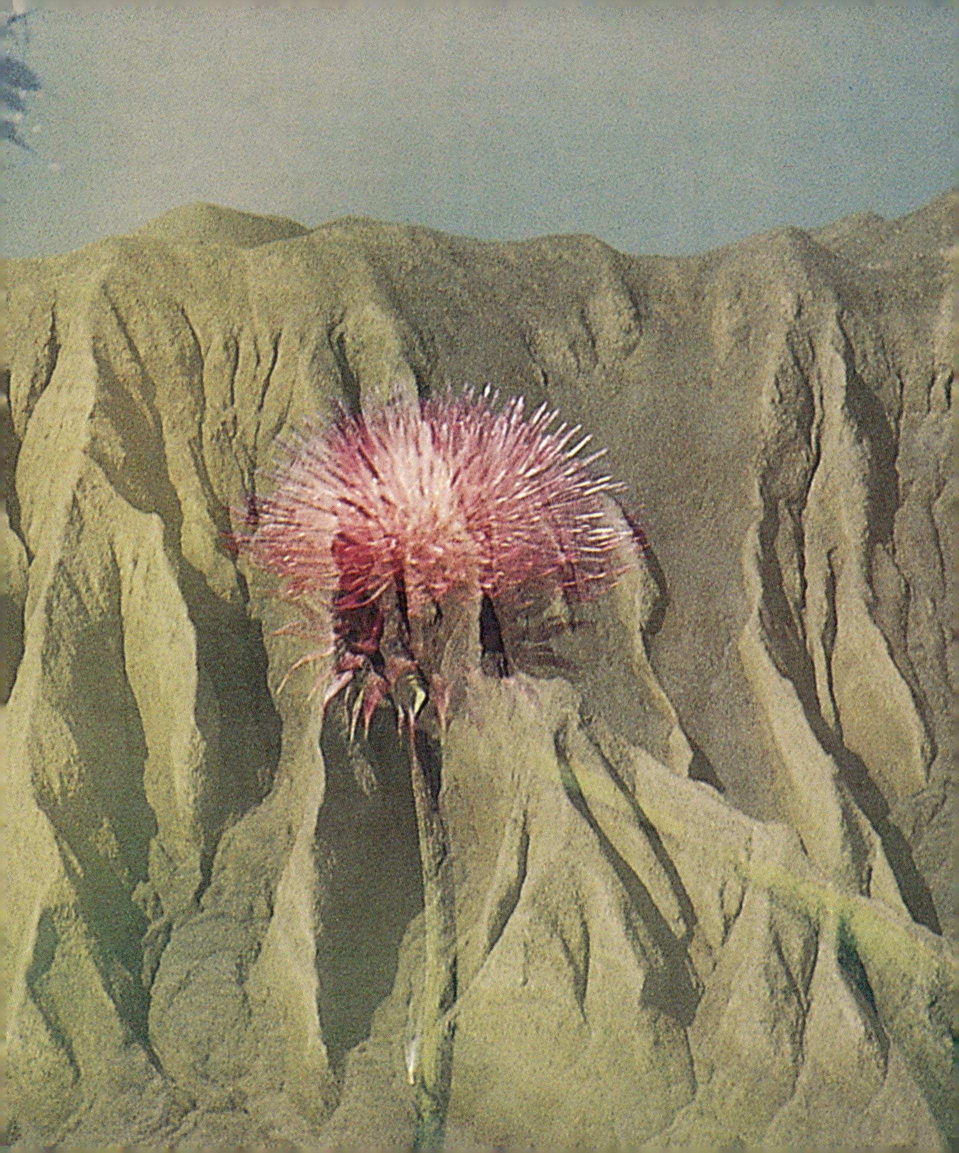

Rainfall is essential to a farmer's success. When the rains did not fall for two weeks, my father was worried. When the third and fourth weeks passed with no rain, I saw his face grow very grave. Not once did he become angry.

The only thing my father did about the drought was pray. Farmers gathered from miles around, at special prayer meetings, filling the little white churches that dotted the rolling landscapes. They called upon God Almighty to save their land and their crops. But for a whole year the Lord was silent. Day after day, the sun bore down on their crops. Then the winds began to blow. And the clear bright air that I enjoyed breathing as a child suddenly became polluted with dust. "That's South Dakota land you are breathing, Son," my father said. When the winds blew harder, the dust sandblasted the few rows of corn that had managed to survive the drought. The fragile young plants, wilted and weakened for want of refreshing water, were no match for the grit driven by the hot winds. There was total devastation.

I watched the river dry up. Little pools of water became mud holes where squirming bullhead catfish died.

If it had been a normal year, my father would have expected to harvest corn that would fill dozens of wagons. That year my father harvested barely a half a wagon of corn, grown on a half-acre of normally swampy ground.

A total disaster? Not quite. For half a wagon of corn was better than none at all. I shall never forget my father's dinnertime prayer that night.

"Dear Lord. I thank You that I have lost nothing this year. You have given me my seed back. Thank You!"

Not all farmers had as much hope as my father did. More than one piece of property was sold on the courthouse steps.

I recall seeing a slogan on a calendar during those tough times: *"Great people are ordinary people with extraordinary amounts of determination."* I'm convinced that that slogan exemplified the positive attitude of my father that inspired his bankers to go along with him and give him an extension on his mortgage. His hope was contagious.

Several years later, good weather came again. Prices rose sharply. Farm products prospered. The mortgage was paid off, and my father died a successful man!

*When faced with a mountain, I will not quit!
I will keep on striving until I climb over,
find a pass through, tunnel underneath—
or simply stay and turn the mountain
into a gold mine with God's help!*

Now may the God of hope fill you with all joy and peace in believing, that you may abound in hope by the power of the Holy Spirit.

ROMANS 15:13